Recorder profiles

JOHN M. THOMSON

Schott London 1972

First published in 1972
by Schott & Co Ltd
48 Great Marlborough Street London W1
Printed in Great Britain by
Caligraving Ltd., Thetford, Norfolk
All rights reserved
ISBN 901938 092

FOR GRETA AND WALTER BERGMANN

CONTENTS

ILLUSTRATIONS

Following page 12

WALTER BERGMANN *and* RENE CLEMENCIC

FRANS BRUEGGEN

FERDINAND CONRAD *and* LANOUE DAVENPORT

CARL DOLMETSCH *and* EDGAR HUNT

BERNARD KRAINIS *and* HANS-MARTIN LINDE

DAVID MUNROW *and* KEES OTTEN

GUSTAV SCHECK

CHRISTOPHER TAYLOR *and* MICHAEL VETTER

Introduction

These profiles were written over a period of several years for the *Recorder and Music Magazine,* when artists visited London for concerts, either on their own or with their groups. When they began, in the early 1960s, such performances were rarer than they now are and the deep interest in medieval, renaissance and baroque music was just beginning. The severe space limitations of a quarterly journal, meant that at times an important theme had to pass by undeveloped, but rather than attempt to change their format I have kept the original shape and invited the subjects to bring them up-to-date.

The information gathered here is not easily obtainable elsewhere and will, I hope, give some picture of the personalities behind the music. Where this is fainter than I would have liked, it may well be that the subject was caught in-between rehearsals, at lunch, or in a Hyde Park deck-chair in the morning sun. Nearly all the artists included have made recordings and some have also a parallel reputation for their editions of recorder and other music.

From the original articles written for the magazine I have selected only those which dealt with recorder players who had at some time been performers and regretfully omitted others involved in different but no less important aspects of the recorder world.

It is appropriate that the publication of these profiles should coincide with the ending of the pioneering era and the welcoming of medieval, renaissance and baroque music, played with increasing understanding and artistry, into our normal musical life.

I am grateful to Ronald E. Corcoran, for many years editor of the *Recorder and Music Magazine* for permission to reprint material and would record his infinite tact, diplomacy and unfailing courtesy. The material for one profile, that of Gustav Scheck, is drawn from a published article by David Lasocki, to whom I make grateful acknowledgment. A full index seemed unnecessary as the sketches are short and those interested in such topics as recorder technique and ornamentation should be able to find the references without undue searching. I have therefore provided an index of names (and groups) only. This, after all, is a book about personalities.

London/Christmas 1971   J. M. THOMSON

RENÉ CLEMENCIC

WALTER BERGMANN

FRANS BRUEGGEN

FERDINAND CONRAD

LA NOUE DAVENPORT

EDGAR HUNT

CARL DOLMETSCH

BERNARD KRAINIS

HANS-MARTIN LINDE

DAVID MUNROW

KEES OTTEN

GUSTAV SCHECK

MICHAEL VETTER

CHRISTOPHER TAYLOR

Walter Bergmann

Wherever recorders exist you are sure to find somebody playing a piece edited by Walter Bergmann. It may be an edition of a work fresh from the British Museum, or an arrangement of folk songs, but whatever the genre, it will have been selected with taste, scrupulously edited and will show an appreciation of the instrument and its needs that has justly earned him a high place in the affections of recorder players. Walter Bergmann has brought to the recorder world high spirited idealism and enthusiasm, combined with the thoroughness and integrity of German scholarship.

British artistic life has been enriched in many ways by Europeans who have settled here since the 1930s. Names distinguished in art, architecture, music and photography spring readily to mind. Walter Bergmann was brought up in Halle, Handel's birthplace, in a family where music was part of everyday life. He was trained as a lawyer in nearby Leipzig, and knew this now grey, forlorn city in the days when Nikisch, Furtwängler and Abendroth made the Leipzig Gewandhaus one of the great orchestras of Europe. His interest in music was always strong, and he became a pianist and flautist, specially interested in chamber music. 'Chamber music is deep in the heart of every German,' he said. On graduation he returned to Halle and law. When the Nazis seized power he was legal adviser to a Jewish firm which came into conflict with the Gestapo. He was arrested, along with other members of the staff, and imprisoned for three months, five weeks of which were spent in solitary confinement. This was an important period. Not only did he make up his mind to emigrate, but he turned to music and started writing poetry. On release, the whole direction of his life changed. In March 1939 he came to England with ten marks and two suitcases, one filled with clothes, the other with music, including the Fantasias of Purcell, a recorder and a flute. At a difficult time he received support from the Society of Friends and was able to bury himself in the British Museum where he studied eighteenth century music.

In 1940, with the fall of France, he was interned for eight months in the Isle of Man, where he made music of every possible kind. Some time after his release he started work at Schott's, as a packer. 'I knew something about recorders, having brought a tenor over with me,' he said. 'I'd found it more suitable for eighteenth century music than a Boehm flute.' Michael Tippett then asked him to be accompanist for his choir at Morley College and also if he would start recorder classes. 'Only very slowly I made my experiments but when I left I had four recorder classes,' he recalled. When Tippett left Morley College, Walter Bergmann moved to the Mary Ward Settlement.

This position stimulated his deep interest in amateur music making of every kind and his special flair for working with children. Since then he has become familiar at a variety of London Institutes, been a regular tutor at Roehampton summer school, closely involved with the Society of Recorder Players, and has moved over the length and breadth of the country, teaching, adjudicating, presenting his own eighteenth century extravaganza *Musical Pills to Purge Melancholy*, playing harpsichord continuo and conducting professionals and amateurs.

Composers he feels most affinity for are Hindemith, Telemann and Purcell, although he describes his own musical temperament as being in close sympathy with Schumann. Hindemith has always been a strong musical influence. Telemann, at first he despised, until suddenly, while playing a quartet he found the right way, with what he describes as the right tempo and balance. Purcell is a great love of the moment and he is also very fond of Blow. Of all the works he has edited he is perhaps proudest of Blow's *Ode on the Death of Purcell* and Jeremiah Clarke's *Ode on Purcell's Death*.

As an editor of recorder music he feels there should never be any compromise in quality—'If you can't do it without a compro-

for Recorders for him which he performed in London in the same solo recorder concert as *Gesti*. *The Times* wrote of its 'novel sonorities . . . swirls, gargles, trills and hiccoughs' and while expressing doubts about the permanence of both the Berio and the Andriesson concluded that these works offered the recorder 'a new lease of musical life'. The most informed opinion was that of Bill Hopkins in the *Recorder and Music Magazine* of February 1967: 'It was Berio's *Gesti* which did most to show what the recorder can mean to a contemporary composer . . . *Gesti* made complete sense as a formal entity; its melodic and dramatic interest were sustained to the end. Its power to excite and to disturb was exactly comparable to that of, say, the trapeze artist at a circus; and if anyone wishes to think that this is what contemporary music is "about", then *Gesti* is decidedly for him. For others, it had the inestimable merit of exploring to good effect techniques and possibilities few would have imagined.'

Frans Brueggen reads widely, especially in modern literature, and in the field of scholarship his special interest is the articulation of eighteenth-century wind music. He has a rapidly growing fine collection of recorders and traverse flutes as well as of seventeenth-century painting and furniture. His intense seriousness as a musician is irradiated by an allusive wit and an individual sense of humour. He has kept alive that happiest of qualities—'an interest in things and about things'—which transcends the often egocentric world of the performer and gives him a quite rare sense of dedication.

René Clemencic

An extraordinary aspect of the early music field today is its pro-
liferation of activities. The finest artists are not content to stay
still, but continue developing, forming new combinations and
programmes as they absorb and so exhaust their interest in a
particular field. This says a great deal for the health of the performing side of our musical culture, even if the more cynical feel our
interest in renaissance and baroque is a counterbalance to contemporary fragmentation rather than something of intrinsic
musical worth. René Clemencic, who for a number of years was
director of the Musica Antiqua, Vienna, and who first visited
Britain for the Deller music festival at Stour, has entered a new
field of activity, that of performing seventeenth-century baroque
opera and church cantatas. To do so he has gathered round himself musicians and singers, amongst whom is the celebrated Rita
Streich, whose voice he considers ideal for music of this period,
with its brilliant, steely tonal qualities. The nucleus of the new
group was his recently formed Drama Musicum in Vienna.

René Clemencic began playing the recorder at school when he
was twelve or thirteen. He started with the piano, but one day
while nervously waiting to sit his exams, a classmate who played
the recorder said to him: 'Let's do something together so you will
be less nervous.' 'We played a small Mozart minuet and from that
moment I was in love with the instrument.' He bought himself a
recorder in Vienna, learned it during the school holidays by
teaching himself so that gradually the recorder absorbed him
more than the piano. He was introduced to his first teacher, Hans
Ulrich Staeps, in an unusual way. During the last days of the
war in 1945 he wanted to hear the Easter music in St Stephen's
Cathedral in Vienna. As the Russians were approaching, it happened that the only music being performed on this day was that
given by the monks themselves. A few days later the Cathedral

was to be burned down. Inside, he met another boy also waiting for the music. It turned out that both of them played the recorder, so the other boy gave René Clemencic his teacher's address, that of Hans Ulrich Staeps. Meanwhile the Russians had occupied the city and it was not until later at a Philharmonic concert under Clemens Kraus, that the boys met again and René Clemencic was introduced to Staeps. Afterwards he studied with Johannes Collette in Nijmegen, followed by Höffer in Berlin, and others.

Apart from building up a career as a concert performer on the recorder he formed and directed the Musica Antiqua of Vienna. Of the many concerts and recordings he feels that one of their finest achievements were performances of *The Play of Daniel* in Cologne, Liege, Ghent, Vienna and Rome. So successful were they in Vienna that the police had to control the crowds after the third night. Some years ago the Director of the Vienna Academy invited him to introduce the recorder to the Academy as a concert instrument, so he taught there regularly until the demands of concert activities compelled him to give it up.

His driving force is now to perform less music than before, but to do it better. He plans two major operas a year, full-scale performances with scenery, of works such as the dramatic oratorios of Antonio Draghi, and an allegorical work, *La Purpura della Rosa*, written by Torrejon in Lima, Peru, in 1701. Draghi lived in Vienna from *c.* 1658 until his death in 1700 and was the first prolific operatic composer of the seventeenth century, writing over sixty-seven pieces. History books compare him to Legrenzi, Stradella and Pallavicino, none of whose operas are performed today. Seventeenth-century opera is little known and it is this which chiefly attracts him. 'I am very interested in the mannered period,' he said. 'We know Monteverdi and now Cavalli, but the others not at all. I find seventeenth-century opera more interesting *dramatically*, before the arias came to play such a role and divided it up. I prefer the Venetian style which is more dramatic and more unified.'

René Clemencic also specialises in contemporary music and at Warsaw in 1969 performed his own work *Meraviglia* ('Wonder'). His repertoire includes Kagel's *Music for Renaissance Instruments*, a work he enjoys playing, 'an incredible combination of composed and improvised music.' This can have from twenty one instruments including crumhorns, trombones, pommer, zinc and portative organ. 'In my own compositions I want to rediscover music as something actual, something born at this moment, instantaneous, but not completely chaotic of course.' Another contemporary work he admires is the Czech composer Ilja Hurník's Suite for recorder, harp and percussion.

At the Vienna Academy he ran a course on improvisation, based on the old masters such as Palestrina, whose highly ornamented motets are particularly relevant. His feeling for improvisation showed itself in the completely fresh way he performed the bird pieces at the Stour Festival. The free aspects of jazz appeal to him and he has played with the clarinettist Fatti George in an intellectual jazz TV show. 'I find jazz musicians better at this than orchestral musicians. They're all performers, much more spontaneous, and their music touches you in a different way. I detest big orchestras. I think they're necessary, but . . . '

He has recently given contemporary music seminars in Europe (where he demonstrates avant-garde techniques such as overtone chords) and the most recent of his own compositions was *Chronos* (Time) given in the Queen Elizabeth Hall, London, on 21 September 1971.

His early music ensemble in Vienna has now changed its name to the Clemencic Consort and recent performances have included a number of concerts of the French rococo by composers such as Boismortier, Couperin and French chansons érotiques, arranged by René Clemencic. He took the recorder classes at Darmstadt when his *Pizzina Nova*, short pieces for two descants, were performed with Gerhardt Braun. He has also recently given the first performance of the oratorio by J. Fux, *Il Testamento di Christo*.

His approach to all the music he plays might be summed up by the title of his own new work, 'when you perform music you have to create *meraviglia* in a very positive sense.'

Ferdinand Conrad

Ferdinand Conrad is a name familiar to English musicians through his fine recordings, his visits to Roehampton Summer School, and more recently, his performances in the Stour Music Festival and London concerts. A musician first and foremost, he sees the recorder as part of the main stream of music, never as an end in itself. He is a teacher, conductor, flute and recorder player and in Germany has pioneered performances of pre-renaissance, baroque and rococo music.

He began his musical studies as a flautist with Emil Prill at the Hochschule für Musik in Berlin, being thrown into the midst of a style of playing that was then popular but which went against his own nature. 'You played very loudly and very fast,' he said, 'it was terrible'. Escaping from this, he found a more congenial style and spirit in the classes of Gustav Scheck, today an eminent figure in the flute and recorder world. He was then the youngest professor of flute in the Hochschule. Conrad studied the modern flute as well as baroque flute. One day Scheck brought a recorder with him to the class and told Conrad to take it away and play it. 'At first I found it very difficult,' he said, but gradually he began to master the instrument. He virtually taught himself the recorder, never having a proper course of lessons. His introduction to the world of early music came when he began playing with a group of musicians under the direction of Fritz Neumeyer. At the end of the 1920s the *Kammermusikkreis Scheck Wenzinger* was formed, with Scheck as flautist and Wenzinger as gambist. This notable group pioneered old music on authentic instruments and Conrad had many opportunities to join them as a recorder player for concerts throughout Europe. He gained invaluable experience in what was then regarded as a highly specialised field. Around 1936 he went with the *Heidelberger Kammerorchester* under Wolfgang Fortner to Paris for performances of the 4th

Brandenburg Concerto, using recorders, a revolutionary move. This was the first time he had played the recorder with Scheck.

After the war Conrad lived first in Lübeck, where many historical buildings had still been preserved, and a city with a feeling for the baroque and rococo in art. When he moved to Hanover, where he now teaches at the Niedersächsische Hochschule für Musik und Theater, he came to a town where nearly everything had been destroyed and a whole new musical life had to be created. 'At first I had to work very hard for old music,' he said. He built up various ensemble groups, taught extensively, began making recordings and giving many broadcasts. He formed his own ensemble, *Kammermusikkreis Ferdinand Conrad*, went on concert tours and organised regular concerts in Hanover. By now, for instance, he has performed all the Brandenburg Concertos, in the second of which he makes an interesting variation of normal performing practice. To help the balance, he sometimes uses three recorders in the first and last movements, with one recorder in the middle movement. Another activity is his Studio for Early Music where pre-baroque music is studied and performed, using recorders, viola da gamba, crumhorns and dulcian amongst other instruments. The intensely demanding work of this period of reconstruction has now brought its reward, for students travel to him from all over Europe. His teaching schedule has become especially heavy with up to thirty lessons a week.

There are differences between the situation in Germany and England. A major problem in Germany is the shortage of good instruments. 'There are so many bad recorders,' said Conrad. 'The so-called "German" fingering was a mistake and we should have kept to the "baroque" (or "English"). Also we haven't enough good teachers and the shortage of instruments is so bad you might have to wait six years to get one from a good maker.'

After his second visit to England he is certain that the English love their recorders—'they call it the queen of all instruments. Here you can play Mozart and similar arrangements without the purists making trouble, and also you have very good modern music.' He does not feel that the recorder can expect to play as significant a part in contemporary music as the flute: 'The recorder is an ancient instrument, it is a diatonic instrument and therefore the opportunities to play modern music aren't as great as with the flute, oboe, clarinet for instance. Although I like playing modern music I prefer it with the flute, not the recorder.'

His own tastes in music are wide and range from Telemann, for technical and virtuoso works, to Handel, Pepusch and Loeillet; with the Italian schools, such as Marcello and Veracini also appealing to him. He has become known as a specialist in baroque ornamentation and wrote a series of articles on the subject for the *Recorder News*. As an authority on early music he arranges many performances of larger works according to baroque performing practice and style. His versions of Purcell's *Fairy Queen* and *King Arthur*, for oboes, recorders, bassoon, cembalo and strings, for instance, have been widely performed, in Herrenhausen, Munich and on the North German radio. He has performed *The Indian Queen* and *The Tempest*, with a chamber orchestra from his Hochschule, under Felix Prohaska, and with the Saltire Singers.

He has practically no leisure time but enjoys painting and drawing, an activity which he shares with his wife. A tall man, he has about him an air of authority, immense dignity, and that warmth of personality that comes through in his playing. He combines the approach of the humanist, the scholar and the born musician.

LaNoue Davenport

LaNoue Davenport, who is tall, lean and rather scholarly looking, has long been associated with the New York Pro Musica. He describes himself musically as 'a sort of latecomer.' He was born in Texas where his father taught him keyboard and the trumpet, and from this beginning LaNoue taught himself dance-band arranging, trying out the results on his friends. 'I put my peers through the awful experience of playing what I wrote,' he said. He was a jazz trumpet player from the age of sixteen and his direction changed when he moved to New York to study and happened to stumble on a course in music history run by a man who was active in early music, Erich Katz. 'It was one of those marvellous history courses where you actually played the music,' he recalled. 'I borrowed a recorder and became fascinated by the music, both by the sounds and by the elements of improvisation that I knew from my experience as a jazz player. Then I became very deeply involved with it and stopped playing the trumpet altogether. I decided this area of music was what I most wanted to explore and about a month later I started teaching the recorder! Eventually I gave concerts in New York with Katz and then formed the Manhattan Consort where we did a great deal of recorder and general music.' He also studied composition in school and graduated from the New York College of Music although he says that he has not written much of his own music for some years.

Pro Musica had been formed by Noah Greenberg in 1953 and although LaNoue Davenport had played in their first concert, when the *Ode on the Death of Purcell* was the main work, he did not join the group as a permanent member until 1960. This took up most of his time and as the group did not go much beyond Schütz and Monteverdi he found himself playing the music of the period he likes best—the renaissance rather than the baroque

—on recorder, sackbult, viol, cornett, crumhorn and other instruments.

The British recorder movement has influenced America a great deal. Not only is the American Society modelled on the English one, but a summer school at Interlochen which LaNoue Davenport started, is run on Roehampton lines. He decided to expand such activities by running two schools, one on the East Coast and one one in the Mid-west. At both, he has concentrated on pushing recorder players into learning other instruments. Students play also the one-keyed flute, the crumhorn and the viola da gamba. The essence of his attitude is that 'The weakness of the recorder movement is the emphasis on the recorder. A whole evening of recorders would be unheard of in the renaissance.'

Crumhorns in particular, attract him: 'I'm mad for the sound! Have you ever heard four crumhorns?' He plays a Steinkopf instrument, with a plastic reed, which is about the same price as a good recorder. However he feels that crumhorns will never become as numerous as recorders. 'They're a little more difficult to play, intonation is a big problem, and they take more physical strength.' A soprano crumhorn instead of a tenor recorder in a consort gives an unusually rich sound.

Music fills most of his life but he is deeply interested in politics ('in *reading* about it') and while travelling always tries to see renaissance and medieval paintings, and the moderns, especially those of Klee and Modigliani. In London he was enthusiastic about the theatre, especially *Oh What a Lovely War*. His musical interests extend to Stravinsky, Berg and Webern and at one time John Cage, leader of the American avant-garde, was his next-door neighbour. 'By knowing John I find that there *is* something to his music and ideas. It's not just Dadaism. Out of all this will come something very worthwhile, for John Cage is a very serious man.' At the same time he admires Bach, but has only a moderate liking for Telemann. Food also interests him. 'It takes on enormous importance when you travel a lot. This search for edible food is really something.' His wife, whom he describes as 'a baroque soprano,' sings in the Manhattan Consort and the Pro Musica.

Pro Musica is still one of the most popular concert attractions on the American scene, giving over 100 concerts throughout the country, in addition to presenting their two medieval liturgical dramas, *The Play of Daniel* and *The Play of Herod*. They have also been in residence over the past few years for two weeks each summer at Stanford University, giving seminars in early music. On his last visit to Britain LaNoue was looking for additional instruments to buy, expecially viols. 'If we have the instruments for people to play then we can have the classes' he said.

He believes that there is at least as much interest in early music in America as in any other country. 'France and Italy are far behind England, Germany and the USA—specially in renaissance music there's much less activity.' During its American tours the Pro Musica finds that many American Universities now have their own groups and there are also many excellent scholars.

Although it may seem a long way from jazz trumpet player to distinguished interpreter of early music, LaNoue Davenport has brought together something from the world of jazz and serious music. The freshness and spontaneity of jazz is a close relation to early music. He has also the humility of the enthusiast. Pro Musica may know a vast amount but it too can learn. 'We go to other people almost as much as people come to us,' he said. 'We wouldn't want to set ourselves up as an authority.'

Carl Dolmetsch

When Arnold Dolmetsch finally returned to settle in England in 1914, harpsichords were still more often than not kept in the 'Fine Arts Department' of museums as examples of a lost craftsman's art and the recorder was considered as obsolete as the serpent. Arnold Dolmetsch had been working in the instrument factories of Chickerings in Boston and Gaveau in Paris and he settled, with his wife and four children, in a house in Hampstead. Soon the Zeppelin raids on London began. Carl, the youngest son, was three at the time, and can still remember sheltering with the family in the cellar, and from an upper window watching a Zeppelin come down in flames. London was no place for a young family, so when in 1917 one of Arnold's pupils, Beatrice Horne, offered him the use of her country house, seven miles from Haslemere, he gladly accepted. In this way began the long and close association of Haslemere with the Dolmetsch family and traditions. 'Here we spent six happy months' recalled Carl. 'Nearby was a Canadian Army camp where my father used to have long talks with the French Canadians and where we were invited to give concerts. When the raids in London became worse Beatrice Horne, who was a brave woman, decided at length she would need her house. This was what led my parents to Haslemere.' The Colonel in charge of the camp made the family removal into a military operation so that children, slow combustion stoves, tools and instruments were all loaded on to army vehicles and taken to their new home.

Although Carl Dolmetsch's name is now so closely linked with the recorder and its renaissance, it was quite involuntarily that he found himself involved in playing, designing or making recorders. His father had acquired an eighteenth-century ivory-mounted treble recorder by Bressan in 1903 and, having taught himself to play with the authentic fingerings from an early English tutor—*Ye Compleat Flute Master*—he included it in his concerts until

1918. At this point it was left on platform seven of Waterloo station by the sleepy Carl, then a child, who was put in charge of the recorder bag while the family waited for their train after a London concert. It was this 'disaster' which sparked off the modern recorder movement, since the loss of his recorder acted as a challenge to Arnold Dolmetsch, who added the manufacture of recorders to the vast array of other 'old' instruments he had built since the 1880s.

'The lost Bressan recorder was found in a junk shop by a friend—who paid the sum of 5/- for it and gallantly returned it to my father. By this time the catastrophe had served its purpose and, as so often happens, had become a blessing in disguise,' said Carl. 'In 1925, when he had subsequently added the production of descant, tenor and bass models to play consorts, he "commandeered" me to learn to play one of the parts.' The following year he was responsible for continuing and developing the entire programme of research and production of all models of recorder. The next surprise for Carl was to be told that, in partnership with his brother Rudolph (already a recorder virtuoso), he was to play one of the recorder parts in the Fourth Brandenburg Concerto, one of the first modern performances of this work with recorders. 'By this time, I was dedicated to the recorder and was given a succession of solos to perform in the ensuing years, including the sonatas by Handel, Telemann, Senaillé and that anonymous best-seller—*Greensleeves to a Ground*.'

The dominant influence in Carl's musical training was undoubtedly that of his father. He was privately educated but when he and his elder brother, Rudolph, felt the need to broaden their experience, Carl studied with various violinists, including Carl Flesch, and Rudolph went to the Royal College, becoming a composer, performer and conductor. 'Rudolph had tremendous versatility,' said Carl. 'If he was given a set task such as playing a work of the greatest difficulty on any instrument he'd play it in three months, perfectly. When the late Frank Arnold asked for a performance of the Bach 6th Suite, for five stringed cello (EAGDC) Arnold entrusted the task to Rudolph.' His virtuosity soon extended to recorder, violin, keyboard, viola da gamba and serpent.

In 1925 when Arnold Dolmetsch was in his late sixties, with a lifetime of arduous touring behind him, a new pattern began .'It's time they came to me' he announced. 'I shall found a Festival.' These early days of the Haslemere Festivals were carefree ones for Carl. 'I used to walk on and off without any nervousness or any sense of apprehension' he said 'whereas it's very different now. There are always hazards, however well you've prepared. Every note the other performers play is also *your* responsibility.' It seemed as if Rudolph would eventually take over from his father, but there were several obstacles in the way. 'My brother had a certain independence of thought' said Carl. 'He didn't want to appear to accept automatically the teaching of his father. He'd become very keen on conducting and had formed his own orchestra in London. My father was rather against the glamour that goes with conducting, and against conductors—it was rather an anti-conductor phobia. Also, my brother had his own recital work, touring as a harpsichordist, and as he was married first he no longer lived at home. I found more responsibility falling on me, simply because I was on the spot.'

Then came the second world war and in 1940 Arnold's death. The Dolmetsch workshops turned from producing instruments to secret aircraft components. 'We found ourselves transferring fine standards of craftsmanship to these mass produced aircraft parts' said Carl. Rudolph went into the services and Carl was retained to direct the workshops. Had Rudolph not enlisted so early he too would probably have been retained for the Haslemere workshops. But in 1942 he was lost at sea. Full responsibility for the Festival, the workshops, and for keeping alive and developing the tradition now fell on Carl.

The post-war years were to be the high water-mark of the recorder revival. Carl had acquired tremendously valuable experience in working with plastics during the war and he now put this knowledge to good use. These were the years of the mass production of plastic recorders, of overseas tours, concerts, lectures, broadcasts, with fresh conquests in the Americas, Europe, and the Commonwealth. On his 1935 American tour Carl had had to explain what a recorder was. Now America has its own movement and its own virtuosos. Carl describes the American approach as 'more glamorous' and American audiences as less inhibited in their reactions.

Carl is still personally responsible for the quality of all instruments issuing from their workshops. 'I check a great deal' he said, 'even though some of the instruments have been voiced by others.' His workers are extremely versatile. 'We don't have anyone grinding away at the same job all the time. Every wood worker can turn his hand to metal work.' Are any new instruments likely to emerge from Haslemere? One writer has suggested they might produce crumhorns. Carl Dolmetsch considers that eighteenth-century oboes might successfully be made—'But it would take time to evolve a modern instrument and put it into production' he said. The great pressure of orders for existing instruments holds him back. 'We're not antiquarians,' he insisted, 'therefore we just don't do something because it's old. I'm not personally interested in an instrument that can't also meet the demands of the modern composer. The recorder successfully spans both worlds. It fulfils all requirements in an uninhibited way.' He has never made medieval recorders because he regards these as being at a more primitive stage of development. If it is to live, the recorder must develop. 'Handel was not tied down to a Henry VIII model, and we shouldn't be tied down to a Handel model.'

How would he like the recorder world to develop in the future? 'More players of virtuoso soloist class' is his first request. 'There are millions of recorder players but the instrument does not *yet* receive in many professional quarters the response that is its due, on a par, say, with the violin, because it's judged on amateur performances. If the violin were judged by amateur standards many unkind things would be said. People also tend to judge the recorder on appearances only and therefore you have the naive assessment of the professionals, and in many cases the critics also. They don't realise the subtleties of producing an instrument which retains that outward simplicity but which is virtually unlimited in what it can produce.' He speaks not only as a recorder player, but as a player of the violin, viol, and sixteen or so other instruments. 'From that position I'm able to say that to play the recorder well is as difficult and requires as many subleties of technique as *any* other instrument.

'I would then like to see the disappearance of that prejudice which bases its assessment of an instrument on its outward appearance and mechanical devices, and also the convention of judging it by whether or not it's been accepted by nineteenth-century orchestras.

'As for the instrument itself, I'd like to find means of producing an orchestral model with a more powerful tone, as powerful as the oboe. Recorder and oboe playing together present no problem, nor is there any with recorder and bassoon.' Improvements he has already incorporated in the instrument are an F sharp key, a device which concentrates and directs the basic tone of the instrument, and a device for producing a diminuendo without loss of pitch.

He feels that recorders could still be exploited more as a *family* of instruments. 'There aren't enough consorts available yet. We can, in fact, do with much more of what we've already been having —sonatas, concertos with orchestras, and consorts.' He frequently commissions contemporary works and finds that those composers who have had an opportunity to know the instrument's true worth are happy to write for him.

The family tradition is continuing. Of his four children, three studied at the Royal Academy, and his eldest son, who is also a professional photographer, teaches and tours in South America, where in his first post he taught history, French, football and the recorder. Carl Dolmetsch's own interests outside music once liberally included pheasant breeding, natural history and gardening. Now they are reduced to two, ornithology and natural history, although he has a lively interest in painting and photography. With more time he would catch up on new movements in the cinema but he manages to see a film only about once a year, usually on board ship. His passion for the recorder, the instrument to which he has particularly dedicated himself, has increased in fervour. 'Anything I or anyone else can do to make it an instrument of greater resource is to be welcomed, provided it doesn't lose what are the very reasons for its popularity, its basic character and charm.'

Edgar Hunt

A characteristic of both recorder and flute is reticence. It is therefore no surprise to find that a man who is an accomplished player of both instruments and a leader of the recorder renaissance in Britain should himself have qualities of modesty which mask the victories his quiet persistence has achieved. Recorder players know Edgar Hunt as the Chairman of The Society of Recorder Players, which he helped found, as the author of the comprehensive *The Recorder and its Music*, as a teacher at Trinity College, an adjudicator, a performer. He is also a practical man, who designs and repairs instruments, a very good shot with a rifle and a skilled compositor. And if one should add another achievement, in a way the most important of all, it was Edgar Hunt who resisted European pressure and tenaciously held this country to what he has called 'English fingering.'

His early years were spent in Bristol, where his father, cathedral organist and string player, also started the Bristol Symphony Orchestra. Perhaps in reaction against his father's preoccupation with strings he was always attracted to wind instruments. He had piano lessons until he was twelve then joined the drum and fife band of his school Officers' Training Corps. 'A Mr Ace, who used to conduct the Zoo Band in Bristol and was Bristol's leading flautist, took an interest in me and helped me to get a proper flute,' he recalls. He then won a flute scholarship to Trinity. 'I liked Trinity from the start,' he said. 'There was a carpet on the stairs and it felt like home rather than a hospital.' This was in sharp contrast with other London schools of music, some of which still resemble public utilities. Until he met Dr J. C. Bridge, discoverer of the Chester recorders made by Bressan, he had never heard of the instrument but the recorder soon began to be as important to him as the flute. At a time of widespread unemployment, the talkies having dispersed the cinema orchestras, he had the good fortune to become understudy to H. A. Chambers, music reader to Novello. 'I'd already started teaching the recorder,' he said, 'but at that time there was no recorder movement. It didn't exist. We were just a few amateurs.'

Finding it hard to obtain cheap instruments for his pupils, he investigated the German market, where recorders with German fingering cost very little. At the *Kasseler Musiktage* in 1934 he found the only maker prepared to use English fingering was Herwig, the others insisted on retaining German fingering which limited the musical possibilities of the instrument. From his small rooms in Dulwich, Edgar Hunt became an importer, and Herwig recorders, with the English fingering he had fought for, began to flow into England, twenty five to a hundred at a time. These were anxious days. 'I had to pay customs duty and always seemed to be in debt,' he said, 'but a solution eventually came when Mr Maynard Rushworth of Liverpool took over the agency and financial responsibility passed from me.'

In 1935 several works, including a tutor, were published, all with an adventurous history, some of which he retells in his book. He became a contributor to a new journal *The Amateur Musician*, and later married the editor, Miss Elizabeth Voss, who had also been in his class at Trinity. With Max and Stephanie Champion, who enlisted the co-operation of Carl Dolmetsch, the Society of Recorder Players came into being in October 1937. 'At these early meetings there were only about thirty to forty of us and we spent most of the time getting in tune.' At about the same time he joined the staff of Schott's.

The recorder was at last treated as a serious musical instrument in London when he began his classes at Trinity. 'I insisted on giving cheap lessons,' he said, 'the total cost for the term being ten shillings, well below the ordinary college fees.' When war broke out, Trinity classes stopped but the recorder enthusiasts still kept going. Edgar and his wife printed a newsletter on their own press until their flat was bombed. Two months later he was in the army.

Edgar Hunt has a gift for teaching: 'In a sense I feel I'm still a student myself, like an officer who has risen *from* the ranks, but who still has sympathy *for* the other ranks.' In music he leans towards composers of the romantic school but applauds the work of the Dutch player Frans Brueggen who has stimulated his own country's composers to write in a contemporary idiom. He would like to publish a complete edition of the works of Anthony Holborne. 'I'm very fond of his way of writing; it's just that little bit simpler and more direct than Dowland and suits the recorder very well.' A founder of the Galpin Society, the learned society which studies the history of musical instruments, author of an unpublished biography of the English musician Robert Lucas Pearsall, he is still bringing into being new projects. He has established a strong link with French players through his Anglo-French recorder courses and he sees this co-operation with a spirited younger generation as an enriching influence on the recorder players of Britain. He has also established links with Germany and Sicily and started a course of baroque music at Trinity College. Some of his pupils are now first-rate performers in their own right, which pleases him, as it must every true teacher.

Bernard Krainis

If Bernard Krainis, the virtuoso American recorder player had become an economist as originally planned, he would surely have been an unusually practical and lucid one, for whatever sphere he entered he would have made a decisive mark. His directness, quick intelligence and far-ranging mind have the spirited and athletic qualities of his music making. He was already experienced on the jazz trombone, piano and violin when he was given a recorder on his twenty-first birthday. 'Fortunately, no one told me it was easy to play so I practised it very seriously', he said. Shortly after the war, when he served in the Air Corps Intelligence from 1943-45, he entered Denver University to study economics, expecting to be able to enjoy the recorder in an amateur way. When offered a Rhodes scholarship in economics he changed his mind. 'I didn't want to do this,' he said, 'so I returned to New York, taking music and musicology at New York University.'

He began teaching very early, 'so as to have people to play the recorder with' and in 1952 made his first recording for Esoteric of four Handel works, the *Fitzwilliam* sonata in D, the sonata in C, the trio sonata in D, and *Nel dolce dell'oblio*. To his astonishment, this early group still reappears under different labels. Like most artists, he is highly critical of his own recordings. Around this time he met up with Noah Greenberg. 'The New York Pro Musica came into existence when Noah Greenberg and I joined forces to present a concert to publicise four recordings we had made independently', he said. 'Noah was the director and I the associate director in charge of the instrumental forces. This association was formed before the records were actually released, however, so we were able to attribute all of them to the " New York Pro Musica". Noah had done Banchieri's *Festino* and an album of Morley works, while I had made the Handel and the Purcell-Blow.' Bernard Krainis's name now appears on many of the group's recordings, such as *The Play of Daniel* and *Music of the Medieval Court*. When the Pro Musica made their first European tour, Bernard Krainis left to become a soloist. As his own career developed he made the Kapp disc of dance music through the centuries, called *Festive Pipes*. 'At this stage of the recorder's career', he said, 'the recording companies felt they had to make something of a novelty of the recorder to catch the wider market, hence the title.' An even more important event was the first appearance of the Krainis baroque trio at Carnegie Hall, New York, on 12 March 1961, with Barbara Mueser, viola da gamba and Robert Conant, harpsichord. He had found it almost impossible to exist as a professional recorder player without a permanent group. 'Proper preparation of baroque music or early music required a close, long term co-operation of specialists that other instrumentalists don't have to face', he explained. 'The recorder needs just the right musical surroundings. It's nearly always chamber music, not soloist's music and you need lots of rehearsals together.' Why a group of three and not four? 'Simply on a logistics level. You can get three people and a harpsichord into a station wagon (American size) and you can't get four.' He has worked several times with larger groups, however, as in the Handel year of 1959, when he gave several concerts.

Since its earliest days he has been deeply involved with the American Recorder Society. He edited their first *Newsletter* and although a professional artist, has always been part of the amateur movement. He feels the American society has now reached a point where it should be primarily concerned with the *quality* of recorder playing. The need to popularise the instrument has passed. 'It is now time to set up the machinery to help people advance', he believes. 'This should be the new aim of the recorder movement.' He is full of positive ideas on how to bring this about through films, postal courses and specialist classes.

Although New York is the home of the Pro Musica and of his own baroque trio, the situation is still far from easy for professional musicians specialising in this field. 'Any performer must face a largely hostile environment,' he said, 'but the early music specialist is confronted by several hazards all his own. These can be listed as (a) no tradition (b) suspicion of concert managers and impresarios for anything different (c) the attitudes of musicologists and critics (d) hall acoustics designed for more brilliant and powerful modern instruments and (e) the poor impression left on concert-goers by well-meaning amateur performances of early music.'

A feature of his playing is his embellishment of certain movements. This is melodic rather than one achieved through using individual ornaments and is based on a careful, sympathetic study of the slow movements of Bach. It is also appropriate to Handel sonatas, the Italian school and a great deal of Telemann. In his approach to ornamentation, again clear cut and intelligent, he begins with the work's basic harmonic and melodic elements. 'After reducing it to this kind of skeleton, you can work out any of these movements, so they have flow, development and shape.' Ornamentation, as an isolated thing in itself, he believes is impossible to teach. He found unexpected corroboration of his methods when working at the slow movement of a Telemann flute sonata which the composer himself had embellished. 'I was glad to see that this confirmed my own approach,' he said, 'though Telemann's style was a little more flowery than mine.' Dissemination of knowledge such as this amongst American recorder players has had a curious result: 'the strange thing is that in the States, the poor benighted, much maligned amateur player now knows much more about eighteenth-century performing style than the average symphonic musician.'

He finds Bach more satisfying than Telemann or Loeillet, and like all recorder players wishes the repertoire was larger. He teaches extensively in America, though he is gradually confining himself to advanced students with professional ambitions. This leaves him with about eight to ten serious students, some of whom he describes as 'really first-rate performers who *insist* on becoming professional musicians'.

Two visits to Britain were made in 1965. At the first, in May, his baroque trio appeared at the Wigmore Hall and on the second, in July, he returned to record a group of concertos with an orchestra conducted by Antal Dorati.

The visit of the trio was particularly important, as it was the first American ensemble specialising in early music (apart from the Pro Musica itself) to perform in London. As a review of the concert in the *Recorder and Music Magazine* said: 'Our age is witnessing the gradual growth of practical performing traditions of the music of earlier periods, which will in time give stability to the interpretation of once extremely shadowy parts of musical history. Bernard Krainis's playing is marked by zest and an outwardgoingness that made a strong impression. This is the positive kind of playing we would like to hear regularly.'

Hans-Martin Linde

Of Handel's *Alexander's Feast*, Bernard Shaw once observed that he had enjoyed it mightily, even though he was sitting on a cane-bottomed chair. Modern performances are rare and at the 1965 Stour Music Festival, although descendants of Shaw's cane-bottom chairs were in use, it was still a rousing, extrovert work, even if, like public meetings, a little long. Tucked away in the orchestra in the Wye Village Church were two celebrated recorder players, Ferdinand Conrad and Hans-Martin Linde, members of a small group of German musicians who had come over specially to play in the Handel, in Purcell's *Come Ye Sons of Art* and in Vecchi's madrigal opera *L'Amfiparnaso*.

Hans-Martin Linde first became interested in early music through his teacher, Gustav Scheck, then at Freiburg. On completing his studies, Linde taught at the Conservatorium in Hagen, Westphalia. While recording a broadcast at the Cologne radio station he met by chance a group of musicians who specialised in early music. Amongst them was August Wenzinger, and the friendship which sprang up between these two men, led to Linde's introduction to the Schola Cantorum at Basle, where he has been a teacher and lecturer since 1957. He is not only concerned with the recorder but also with the baroque transverse flute and he conducts the vocal ensemble of the Schola. This choir is often combined with an Early Baroque Orchestra of three instrumental groups for performances of works by the Italian masters. He lectures too on interpretation in early music, at the Academy.

An extremely versatile musician, he often plays the baroque one-keyed flute and the modern Boehm instrument. On his concert visit to London in 1967, David Lasocki asked him whether he found the baroque flute more difficult than the modern instrument*. His reply showed why he has such affection for
Recorder and Music Magazine, London, May, 1967.

43

the older flute: 'Some passages are very tricky on the old flute, for example the Badinerie from the B minor Suite by Bach which you could probably play after your first three lessons on the modern flute; but often as in Handel sonatas, it is just as easy, if not more so. Anyway the whole atmosphere and conception is just right—I like it, it is such a warm, human instrument.'

The concert group of the Schola Cantorum plays a semitone lower than modern pitch, the same as that used at Leipzig in Bach's time. 'The baroque flute I have actually plays at modern pitch, but I had an extra-long upper-middle-piece made for me in order to play at the lower pitch. I have two treble recorders at the two pitches'. Also in conversation with David Lasocki he described what he thought were the greatest recorder works: 'Of course there are the Brandenburgs—and the Bach cantatas . . . the *Actus Tragicus* . . . *Himmelskönig, sei willkommen.* . . . I don't get a chance to play them very often, but when I do it's marvellous! The Handel sonatas I think are rather over-rated. The C major is good . . . the A minor . . . but the G minor and F major I don't like very much. There is the D minor *Fitzwilliam* sonata—but I like that better on the flute, and anyway you get two extra movements there! But Telemann—Telemann I really am fond of. Telemann is *the* recorder composer. The A minor Suite, that wonderful quartet for recorder, two flutes and continuo from the *Tafelmusik*—and the D minor sonata.'

He has composed several works for recorder, a sonata in D, a trio for recorder, flute and harpsichord, and a capriccio for three recorders, three strings and percussion. His recent set of *Fantasies* and *Scherzi* for recorder solo use special effects, besides flutter tonguing and vibrato. He has edited new editions of Telemann, Handel, van Eyck and other old masters. Like most virtuosi he is always looking for new works and wishes German composers would respond as the Dutch have to Brueggen. One specially written for him is Rudolph Kelterborn's *Scènes Fugitives*: 'It's twelve tone, and is for recorder and large orchestra' said Hans-

Martin Linde. 'It's very happily instrumented so that there's no moment, even in a big hall, when you can't hear the recorder. I've done it several times and think it's a very good piece.'

He is specially interested in phrasing and articulation. 'I normally find that too many recorder players are not really concerned with the playing of wind instruments,' he said. 'There are different nuances in the forming of the tone. Too many recorder players have too few methods of articulation. I concentrate on this with my pupils at Basle. Like all old instruments, including harpsichords, where the player cannot command much variety of dynamics, he has to make his playing interesting. With my students I find that whereas most of them have *quick fingers*, their playing is often extraordinarily boring because there are no nuances in the articulation.'

Vibrato also concerns him. 'Sometimes there are discussions about the tone of the vibrato', he said. 'Some people say the recorder must be played without any, or with just a little vibrato. Although I know that in earlier periods the vibrato was like an ornament, I think we must look on the recorder not only historically, but we must try to bring it into balance with other modern instruments. The good recorder player must therefore have various degrees of vibrato, ranging from the barely perceptible upwards, and always suiting the nuances of individual styles of interpretation for solo playing, ensemble, medieval, high baroque and modern.'

At the Stour concerts he used an ivory recorder made by the late Hans Conrad Fehr, a Swiss, whom he described as being very popular on the Continent. The ivory makes for a heavy instrument, but one tending towards a more brilliant sound, slightly louder than that given by wood. Linde also likes using Coolsma and von Huene instruments.

Although Fehr himself has died, Linde finds that the quality of his recorders has improved as his workers have had time to make experiments and their instruments have become consistently good.

In 1967 Linde was first flute with the Cappella Coloniensis on their Polish tour. In Warsaw he and his friend Günther Höller played the Telemann concerto for flute and recorder.

'After the last movement there was tumultuous applause! We had to come back and repeat it again and again for them. Well, we thought, we are good, but not *so* good, and we really couldn't understand it. But afterwards we were told that the Polish tunes which Telemann used in this movement can still be heard in Poland today, and that's why the audience loved it so much. I think this showed that he really penetrated to the people when he visited Poland.'

Although Frans Brueggen and Hans-Martin Linde are good friends they are never invited to play together 'People seem to think that we are sworn enemies, but in fact we get along together very well.' When they both took part in the course at Saratoga Springs in the USA in 1965 they played several works together, including the Telemann concerto for flute and recorder: 'It was simply wonderful! Nothing needed to be said—everything went so smoothly'.

He reads a great deal and is deeply interested in art, being a painter himself and a collector of works by young contemporaries. An intense, highly-charged personality, a combination of virtuoso and scholar, a special twentieth-century kind of musician, he follows in direct descent from the pioneer work of Scheck and Conrad. His central position at Basle has given him an excellent platform for the dissemination of fresh and beneficial views.

David Munrow

If we live in another country we are likely to see life from a different angle. Sometimes the experience brings special insights into behaviour and all the arts that will throw fresh light on the patterns of human development as happened to Darwin, the anthropologist Evans-Pritchard, collectors of flora and fauna and even to collectors of folk song. When Maud Karpeles and Cecil Sharp explored the isolated mountain area of the Appalachians in America they discovered a source of folk song that had closer parallels with the England, Ireland and Scotland of the seventeenth-century than with the twentieth. This was their richest find. On another level, when the anthropologist Claude Lévi-Strauss left France to take up the chair of sociology in the University of Sao Paulo in Brazil he came into contact with the Indian population of the interior. The direction of his life changed. He began to study primitive culture, especially their modes of thought and behaviour and was able to use these insights to formulate general concepts that illuminate all societies.* David Munrow would not suggest that his stay in South America as a student teacher for the British Council was as yet of equal importance, but there is no doubt that this experience has stimulated him into a most coherent and persuasive approach to the performing traditions of early music.

It was a German student who had digs in his house who introduced him to the recorder. 'I would sit at the bottom of the stairs and listen to him playing. He lent me his recorder and music so that when the competitions came up at school I borrowed his recorder and beat all these people who'd been learning other instruments for years. It was rather embarrassing. My parents then bought me a set of recorders and encouraged me to take up

*See especially Claude Lévi-Strauss's *The Savage Mind* (Weidenfeld), and his inaugural lecture, *Scope of Anthropology* (Cape), paperback.

47

the bassoon, which I learnt from Vaughan Allin of the City of Birmingham Symphony Orchestra, a very fine player. But I found myself getting more and more interested in the recorder.'

He then spent a year in South America at Lima on the British Council student teacher scheme. He travelled over 10,000 miles by land and came into contact with a tremendous amount of folk music. 'I dimly realised that this was all mixed up with instruments and traditions mostly dead in Western Europe. For instance, when the Spaniards came to South America the Indians copied their instruments and incorporated them into their music. I found renaissance flutes and recorders, cylindrical of course, because they were made of bamboo. The Indians had gone on using them ever since without altering them a scrap.'

He listened especially to the Indian tribes in the Andes who played a simple, straightforward kind of music, using the pentatonic scale. 'It was deeply moving: and when one looked at their conditions of life, rather disturbing. There was a very great sadness, nearly everything was in a minor key. By contrast, in Lima, you had the creole music; a bastard form of Spanish folk music, similar to Flamenco; brilliant, virtuoso.' From these experiences came his belief that the essence of an early music performing tradition might be found in folk origins, rather than in the tradition of western classical music. This coincides with a view expressed as long ago as 1957 by Anthony Baines in his *Woodwind Instruments and their History*: ' . . . in the quieter, remoter parts of the Continent, medieval wind instruments live on today as folk instruments, unchanged save perhaps for a small modification here, or a sign of degeneration there . . . Here is material of real importance. . . ' 'It is not difficult for a student of violin to find teachers and virtuosi for his instrument. But those looking for models in medieval and renaissance music find it hard,' he said. There are, of course, many hints in the surviving instruction manuals, such as Ganassi, and these are useful guides. Ganassi recommends the study of singing and with this advice David

Munrow wholeheartedly agrees: 'I spend more time listening to singers and what they do with their voices than anything else. All players should sing—so much of the early music is vocal. After this, one should look to folk players rather than to those who are just finding their way with these instruments after a gap of 400 years.'

He played a recording which he described as *the* most beautiful woodwind sound. It was not medieval music nor a modern flautist or recorder player but a performer on the Roumanian *nai*, a kind of syrinx or panpipes. The freshness, crispness and edge to the sound in this 'Cintec de Dragoste' or 'Song of Love' appealed to him enormously. 'It has a vital improvisatory quality. Later music can't have it because it isn't improvised.' He also gets inspiration from singers like Cleo Laine, or equally, Alfred Deller. 'I like so many different singers it's hard to know where to begin.'

In Morocco he once met a shepherd out in the countryside. 'We had no language in common,' he said, 'but this man sat down and played the instruments I was carrying in my pack, then walked away and back to his sheep. He was one of the few untutored and indubitably great artists I've ever met. It's experiences like this that makes me think such a player gives one a closer link with renaissance or medieval sound.

'I believe early music is expressive. One reads in books of people being moved to tears. Music must always have produced a direct emotional effect. Listeners were not at a concert but at a mass, or aristocratic function, or private gathering. The problem is not the same expressiveness as Beethoven or Chopin dynamics but something not immediately apparent in music. I'm still looking for it, but I get closer by looking at folk music and folk instruments than by looking at music written after 1600, with the beginnings of opera and the foundations of the modern orchestra.'

After Lima, David Munrow read English at Cambridge—'I spent three years industriously making music and not doing any work.' This included singing in the Jesus College Chapel Choir. With Charles Cudworth he gave the first modern performance of William Boyce's *Cambridge Ode*. Thurston Dart started him on the crumhorn and he was stimulated by fine players such as Don Smithers on the cornett and all windcap instruments. He met Christopher Hogwood who has been his harpsichordist ever since. When Cambridge ended he did research into seventeenth-century bawdy songs at Birmingham University and went into teaching.

He started giving lecture recitals on early woodwind instruments and their music and played a crumhorn part specially written by Richard Rodney Bennett for *Timon of Athens* at Stratford-upon-Avon. 'After two terms' teaching I decided the only thing I wanted to do was play. I was offered a job in the Royal Shakespeare Theatre Wind Band playing the bassoon, recorder, crumhorn and rauschpfeife.' He also taught early woodwind instruments for a year under the late Thurston Dart at the recently formed music department of Kings College, London. He lives in St. Albans, a good base for his proliferating concerts, recordings and TV appearances.

After concerts in February 1967 with James Bowman, Oliver Brookes, Christopher Hogwood and Mary Remnant, David Munrow felt that he had found a lively combination of performers to form a consort. 'We all decided it would be a good idea if we went on working together. We got a Monday concert after a BBC audition and since then everything has snowballed a bit.' He speaks appreciatively of his artists—'It's marvellous, for instance, to have a counter-tenor like James Bowman, who has a hard masculine sound capable of great expressiveness.'

He brings back instruments from his travels so that in his house he has an intriguing collection. These include the early instruments he uses in his recitals—Steinkopf replicas and others ranging from North Africa through Japan to the Andes. Sometimes he has to work on an instrument for two years or so until it plays properly.

His collection is alive, everything is playable and is played—'It's not like a gigantic toyshop.'

He would like composers to write for the recorder and for the other early instruments, for 'no instrument is really alive if neglected by the living artist.' He feels there could be an enormous future in the avant-garde and in pop for those with an individual sound. 'I deplore the lack of good modern recorder music and think that Berio's piece the best thing that's happened to recorder music in the twentieth-century.'

His various activities complement each other so that if he lectures on Machaut at Leicester it seems part of the same process of discovery and experimentation. 'The marvellous thing about my life is that I'm earning my living doing something I like. I've seen so much that's wonderful in early music.'

At their Wigmore concert they played English music with a stunning sense of style and sympathy for the nuances of the words so it was no surprise to hear him say that he loved almost all English music, especially Purcell, who was probably his favourite composer. 'I even like Elgar', he added, '*Falstaff* especially, and of modern English music, everything from Britten to Richard Rodney Bennett'. He is always exploring folk and primitive music and this cross-fertilisation of early music is an imaginative breakthrough of the first order.

Kees Otten

Kees Otten has no time for the conventional. A pioneer of the Dutch recorder movement, he must be one of the few players to have performed in a cabaret, to have been a dance-band leader and a devoted fan of jazz. Warm, open and impulsive, his Roehampton classes were always popular.

As a boy he had his first recorder lessons from an uncle, Willem van Warmalo, playing a very cheap German instrument, with German fingering. Before the war he wanted to be a jazz musician, Jelly Roll Morton and the Red Hot Peppers being his heroes. When he entered the Amsterdam Muzieklyceum, where his mother taught the piano, his direction changed. He became a clarinet student and could eventually be found playing Brahms sonatas at evenings of house-music. 'I wanted to play only long-hair music then,' he said, 'I was very snobbish.' He again took up the recorder, managing to continue his studies throughout the war, until afterwards the interest in jazz returned. He played clarinet and alto-sax in a dance band, then more astonishingly did a cabaret act with the recorder, in which he imitated the violin and other instruments, achieving what Edgar Hunt has described as 'an astonishing *glissando* effect.' He hesitated still between jazz and serious music, especially when invited by Kid Dynamite, a negro band-leader, to sit in with his band and tour with him. The issue was decided when the Dutch harpsichordist Hans Brandt Buys asked him to play the recorder for broadcasts of Bach Cantatas. 'I was a little fed-up with the atmosphere surrounding jazz music,' commented Kees, 'so I started to play more serious things.' He became a teacher at the Lyceum, beginning with many classes of children.

Carl Dolmetsch's 1946 Dutch tour confirmed him in his choice of instrument and career. 'I learned very much in the way of good recorder playing,' he said, 'and became a specialist in the recorder. I think this was the first time in Holland.' He changed over completely to an instrument with English fingering. A meeting with Joannes Collette, an excellent recorder player from Nijmegen, was also important and he now felt he wanted to give the recorder an official place in Dutch musical life. As the Muzieklyceum was not an official institute, he could experiment with classes for professional recorder players. The classes were successful and grew in size and the recorder began gaining official recognition. There are now three professional teachers at the Muzieklyceum, including Frans Brueggen, a former pupil. Dutch recorder players can find good teachers in many towns and can take three nationally standardised examinations. Now exactly the same is possible for recorder players as for violinists. It is unfortunate that in Holland, children still use German fingering on descant recorders manufactured within the country. Kees often would prefer to begin with English or 'baroque' fingering. He teaches now in Amsterdam, Rotterdam and Utrecht.

His Amsterdam Recorder Ensemble, a quartet founded in 1949, introduced Dutch audiences to early music and to new works, some in the twelve tone system being specially written. The range was further widened when he founded the *Muziekkring Obrecht*, in 1952, which concentrated on music of earlier periods by composers such as Guillaume de Machaut and Dufay. He then formed the *Syntagma Musicum*, which has broadcast many different radio programmes using viols, fiddles, crumhorns and similar early instruments. Their first record won an Edison award. They have toured throughout the world.

He hates playing to audiences who sit like tailors' dummies—'I like it so much in England that people are able to laugh. They listen joyfully and there's always a nice mixture. It's very difficult in Germany and Holland. They listen to *Till Eulenspiegel* as if it was the *St Matthew Passion*.' His impressions of England include surprise at the strength of the English recorder movement and surprise that although tutors have differing styles and interpre-ative views, they can remain good friends. 'It is not a kind of politics,' he said. 'This is very important I think, for Holland.'

As a teacher, he believes in letting students discover solutions for themselves. 'I like them to take shakes and so on in their own way. I try to draw them out and not impose my pattern on them. I try to explain very much with words, rather than play for them, so that by using another medium, they have to work it out for themselves.' His approach to the recorder has changed. 'When I was about twenty I wanted to be a virtuoso, to be the fastest recorder player in the world. At the moment I'm not very interes-ted in it. I now like to play the slow movements. I try to get the maximum expression with as many kinds of vibrato, tone, phrasing as possible. You must always give to the audience something musical.'

He has written articles on his instrument, composed studies for it and edited a recorder series. Specially known for his performances of contemporary music, he has had several Dutch composers, including Henk Badings, write for him. Although constantly touring, he likes best to be at home with his two young sons, Willem Jan, and Michiel. His very cosmopolitan approach to the recorder and its music sweeps aside narrowness and the fustian. He does not hesitate to learn from what we might feel are the most unlikely of sources such as a good cabaret act with an artist like Danny Kaye. In one respect his musical taste has remained constant. If he had to go to a desert island, he would take Bach—'definitely not Vivaldi!'

Gustav Scheck

Gustav Scheck is a legendary figure in the recorder world, a distinguished pioneer of the revival of the baroque flute and an equally remarkable teacher of such fine performers as Ferdinand Conrad and Hans-Martin Linde. Born in Munich in 1901 he studied musical theory, piano and flute at school and went on to devote himself to medical and musical studies. He reached a point where he had to choose between becoming a doctor or a musician. Although spending around nine hours a day practising the flute he passed his school leaving exams and went on to medical school. We can be thankful that in the end music had the stronger pull—he abandoned medicine and went to study musicology with Professor Wilibald Gurlitt and the flute with Richard Roehler.

His interest in flutes had begun early. In a short extract from his autobiography* he said: 'In my former life I must have been a golden oriole, I am so mad about flutes. At the age of ten I bought myself a piccolo. I had heard and seen two players in the school orchestra perform on these curiously-fashioned wooden tubes in the priests' march from Mendelssohn's *Athalia*. Previously I had taken violin lessons but now the wonderful sounds of these flutes sank into my soul. For days it was as if I had been bewitched —I went around in a dream . . . A year later when I was searching for a flute method in a music shop I found the Theoretico-Practical Flute Tutor of Richard Roehler. Timidly I asked whether anyone gave lessons in flute playing. 'Aye, that one' said the Freiburg music dealer, indicating the writer of the tutor. At which I respectfully asked, 'Is the author still alive then?' for I could not believe that such a great man could possibly be with us here and now.' While studying musicology with Gurlitt, Scheck worked hard with Roehler.

Recorder and Music Magazine, London, May, 1968, translated by David Lasocki.

Gustav Scheck

It was in Gurlitt's Institute that he first got to know the recorder
—Peter Harlan's copies of Dolmetsch instruments. In 1929 he
gave his first treble recorder recital in which he played (apprehen-
sively he recalls) the baroque flute in a Hasse concerto and the
recorder in Bach's Brandenburg 4. 'When I stepped up before the
German Radio Symphony Orchestra to play Telemann's A
minor Suite, the musicians laughed about "the instrument for
children." But they were unprejudiced enough to alter their
opinion at once and show delight.' Later Scheck introduced the
recorder as a new subject at the Berlin High School of Music and
played it in the Brandenburg Concertos with the Gewandhaus
Orchestra.

In 1930 there began his distinguished partnership with the
cellist and gambist August Wenzinger and the harpsichordist
Fritz Neumayer. Together they formed a chamber trio and a
twelve-piece orchestra the *Kammermusikkreis Scheck-Wenzinger*
which specialised in playing old music on original instruments at
low pitch. These groups became very popular in Germany and
were vital for the growth of the popularity of the recorder and for
the revival of early music. Four years later he reached a highly
influential position as flute teacher at the famous Berlin Hochschüle
for Music. It was during the 1930s that he became internationally
famous as a flautist. Scheck opposed the Nazi regime and often
his group gave concerts in churches and cathedrals as a form of
protest. After being denounced by some of his pupils the trio
was compelled to disband in 1942. He then underwent a period of
great hardship during which his wife nearly died. At the end of
the war he possessed only a flute and copies of the Mozart flute
concertos in a rucksack.

After the war he began a new life when in 1946 he founded the
Hochschule for Music in Freiburg which was soon to become the
base for training a new generation of recorder and flute players.
He had chosen Freiburg because of its proximity to the borders of
France and Switzerland. Besides the normal curriculum the school

specialised in old music and instruments as well as in contemporary developments. Scheck brought to the school extremely high standards and attracted an international body of students, many coming from the far ends of the earth. His dominant interests were cited when in 1950 the University of Freiburg awarded him an honorary doctorate 'for services rendered to the music of Bach and his contemporaries'. He spent eighteen years as principal and when he retired devoted himself to touring, teaching and working on a book on the flute and flute-playing.

He had toured widely throughout his long life but until 1968 had never visited England. With Walter Bergmann on the harpsichord, in January he gave two concerts in the Purcell Room on the South Bank. Of his recorder playing Stanley Sadie wrote in *The Times*: 'He produced that crisp, cool tone that sets the lines of baroque music in the necessary sharp profile: not much emotion, but clarity, brilliance and point. The Handel A minor sonata went particularly well, done with vivacity and with nicely-placed ornaments in the Adagio; and in Loeillet's pleasantly fluent piece his passage-work was specially spirited'. Stanley Sadie went on to describe the Leonardo Vinci sonata for baroque flute as 'the most forward-looking item in the programme, with its soft, gracefully-sighing lines—the instrument's delicate but warm, even voluptuous tone caught the atmosphere of that new world of musical emotion which was soon to displace the baroque. I particularly liked Mr Scheck's progressively richer embellishments of the opening Siciliana, so closely parallel in sense to rococo scrollwork.' Scheck also gave two master classes at Fenton House in Hampstead, both of them crowded.

His decisive influence as a teacher has included Ferdinand Conrad, Hans-Martin Linde, Hildemarie Peter amongst recorder players and also the flautists Hans-Peter Schmitz and Elaine Schaffer. When LPs began in the 1950s he made eighteen recordings for the Deutsche Grammophon Archiv label, a remarkable series, unfortunately now deleted. It was Scheck's performance in the Brandenburg 4 that introduced me to the recorder in this work, an unforgettable experience that happened in a small record shop in Wellington, New Zealand, tucked away amongst Chinese greengrocers and shabby, downtown shops.

He has used many different makes of recorders throughout his life and for a number of years played on fine ivory trebles by his pupil, the late Hans-Conrad Fehr, who once made a low-pitch instrument for him at only a few days notice. Fehr recorders are noted for their rather reedy tone, which is powerful enough to penetrate the orchestra. He also played for many years on a baroque flute by the celebrated Potsdam maker Kirst, *c*. 1750, but the instrument has now gone back to the collector who lent it.

Since the return of his baroque flute and the disbanding of his trio after the war he has used the flute mainly for contemporary music, believing strongly that it has an important role to play in the present day scene. In baroque music he has specialised in the decorative style developed by Quantz and his concerts are remarkable for their spontaneous and effective improvisation. In his teaching of pre-baroque music he used Ortiz's *Tratado* on the art of playing divisions which he considers important but neglected, as a basis for courses on vocal ornamentation. 'Ganassi seems more a scheme than a practical method' he believes.

In the little time he has away from music he studies the literature of world religions and has a special interest in architecture and painting, stimulated by being married to a painter. He has a deep interest in all the arts and will still take up something new such as a course in phonetics. His life has spanned the important years of the early music and recorder revival; without him it could never have taken such firm and lasting root.

Christopher Taylor

Christopher Taylor is both professional flautist and recorder player, but given the state of things in Britain, inevitably he is heard more often as a flautist. Several years ago in Handel's *Richard I* at the Wells he delighted audiences with his sopranino recorder obbligato. The old days when a famous diva would take her own flautist around the world with her are gone, but were they still here it is likely that Christopher Taylor would be called upon. His operatic experience includes playing the demanding flute obbligato in *Lucia di Lammermoor* for Joan Sutherland at the first performance at Covent Garden and on TV, one of the most brilliant and demanding in the repertoire. The first night coincided with his recording of the Bach Brandenburg Concertos numbers 2 and 4 for Menuhin and the Bath Festival Orchestra. (Christopher and his brother Richard had played the 4th together at the very first Bath Festival.) In changing his embouchure from recorder to flute he was fortunate in that the famous flute solo does not occur until the third act, so his lip muscles had time to adjust. 'The difficulty in switching from recorder to flute is in centring the embouchure' he said. 'On this occasion I had time to blow in, as it were, during the first two acts.' From the depths of the pit to the stage is far enough to cause some anxiety and he was understandably nervous on such an occasion. Morevoer, as the conductor's beat tended to be slow he had to find a sure way of keeping in time with the singer. 'I used to listen to Joan Sutherland's breathing' he explained 'and this gave me the cues I needed.' He finds singers appreciative of his role in the success of such arias: they usually make a point of thanking him.

This opera experience came after an already colourful career. Christopher Taylor began playing the recorder when about thirteen and two years later also took up the flute. He and Richard learned on the same instrument and both tied for first place in a scholarship at the Guildhall, the most valuable part of which was two year's tuition with Geoffrey Gilbert. At this stage Christopher had been playing only a year. At eighteen he was called up and went into the Grenadier Guards where he became a master at playing regimental marches and Palm Court waltzes. He gained useful experience in transposition, for much of the music was written for D flat, E flat and F flutes. At the time the wind section had several talented players including Ronald Waller, bassoon and James Brown, horn. The string section, which included Hugh Bean and Carl Pini, often played in the Palaces and for State receptions, when the wind would join them.

While still a Guardsman, but living at home, he diversified life with Irish dances on the piccolo for the Hammersmith Irish Club, and an interest in jazz led him to take up the tenor sax and clarinet. In 1949 he could be found in the pit of the Hackney Empire playing four instruments and earning £8 a week for twelve shows. 'It was very hard work' he said, 'we played twice nightly and it nearly killed me, lugging all the instruments there and back across London.'

From the Army he went into the BBC Concert Orchestra, playing second flute and piccolo. At this time he began playing recorder consorts with his father's group.* He composed a trio for flute, clarinet and horn which was played at a New Music Society Concert in 1954 by Geoffrey Gilbert, Stephen Waters and Denis Brain. After a year as piccolo with the London Philharmonic he became first flute at the Garden under Kubelik. 'I like playing for opera and becoming part of something that's more than just the orchestra' he commented. From here he moved to the Royal Philharmonic, playing principal when Geoffrey Gilbert was

*The Stanley Taylor consort (see *RMM*, February 1965) was an important post-war professional recorder ensemble. Stanley Taylor played the solo treble part for the dove in Britten's *Noye's Fludde* in the first performance at Aldeburgh, one of the most imaginatively written recorder parts in the whole literature.

absent and, enjoying it under Beecham: 'he had a marvellous way of making you want to play.' Their present chief conductor, Rudolf Kempe, he also admires—'he has a fine stick technique.'

Although he has played recorder fairly often in the opera house and at Aldeburgh, Bath and elsewhere, he finds it somewhat frustrating. Often when the score demands a recorder (as in Handel's *Saul* at the Garden) it is not used, on the grounds of the extra expense. There is still not enough work or opportunity to keep a professional recorder player afloat in London. If you like the instrument, as Christopher Taylor does, you may find yourself learning the difficult Vivaldi concerto for sopranino only to give one performance (for Joseph Horowitz at the Camden Festival) then never playing it again. Apart from the obvious financial waste and artistic frustration there seems a lost opportunity here for a recording to be made. Record companies are still reluctant to use an English name for recorder works.*

His musical experience keeps on growing for he has recently become interested in Indian music and plays flute with John Mayer's 'Indo-Jazz Fusions' group, making with them last year a best-selling jazz LP called 'Indo-Jazz Suite.' Their scores are based on raga techniques and tala rhythmic forms and they use sitar and tabla, improvising with the raga as a basis. The group comprises the Joe Hariot quintet and a quintet led by the Indian composer and musician, John Mayer.

Christopher Taylor specially enjoys playing Monteverdi and Bach on flute and recorder; as an orchestral musician he likes Brahms and Ravel. Although a gentle, quietly spoken man whom you might think would prefer walking, reading and fishing as hobbies, he enjoys motor racing and runs a vintage Aston Martin, a short chassis 1934 sports. He collects antiques—his home is furnished with them—and will admire such things as the monumental brass taps to be found in Victorian bathrooms. He has two

*Not so in 1971, when a variety of English players are featured on recordings.

children, a boy and a girl, both musical. He leads a very busy life freelancing for orchestral playing as well as film work. In the Robert Bolt *A Man for all Seasons* he joined the Stanley Taylor consort to play seventeenth-century pastiche music composed by a Frenchman. But if you really want to hear him at work, go to a James Bond film when more than likely he'll be doing the flute parts. If you see Elizabeth Taylor in *The VIPs* you will hear him playing the recorder. He has also taken up the crumhorn, which he played in the film *Lock Up Your Daughters*. A highly experienced, versatile and accomplished musician, Christopher Taylor has been important in the establishment of the recorder as a normal professional instrument. One wishes that our revival had advanced far enough to allow him even greater opportunity.

Michael Vetter

As an explorer of the outer limits of the recorder's technique and repertoire, Michael Vetter's discoveries will probably take years to absorb. He has extended the range of the recorder without altering its fundamental structure and has given us a new tonal palette supported by tutors and recordings of considerable erudition and brilliance. He has encouraged the younger generation of avant-garde composers to write for him, thus stimulating a new wave of works. His first visit to London in November 1970 clearly demonstrated his skill with children and extraordinary capacities for improvisation on solo treble in his own *Aulodien*, sixty minutes of concentrated music without interruption. This work has recently been re-titled as *fuenota*, Japanese for 'Song of the Flute'. Philosopher, former theologian as well as performer and composer, he has a peculiarly German combination of gifts.

Michael Vetter, still in his late twenties, began his musical ascent in a normal way, when at six he took lessons on the recorder from respectable lady teachers against whom he always seemed to find himself struggling. On Sundays he played small baroque pieces with his father who teaches today at the Münster Musikhochschule. Both parents were musical, his father had been a well-known singing teacher from 1930 to 1960, and a conductor during the war. His mother had sung in an opera group directed by his father. Around the age of 15 he started to play the cello but his extremely poor eyesight made score reading at such a distance too difficult. He began painting, which he took seriously, and writing poems. 'I saw you must work if you do something like this' he said. He was encouraged by his teacher in painting and poetry, but strangely enough his family did not ever envisage his doing serious work in music. He began to be interested in modern music, influenced by his father, a good historian, who felt that such teaching should always be directed towards the present. 'I remember my first concert when I was twelve, with the Henze Piano Concerto', said Michael Vetter. 'Most people didn't like it at all so I said to everyone who thought it was terrible "No, I like it very much". I also disliked it, but I thought I must come to understand it.' In 1957 he wrote to the English composer Arnold Cooke saying he wanted to learn more about difficult and significant contemporary music for recorder and orchestra as Cooke's concerto was the only piece he knew. Out of this friendship grew Cooke's *Suite 1960* and *Serial Theme and Variations*. In 1960 he wrote to Jurg Baur to ask him to compose a piece for him—'he was the only modern composer I knew personally. I'd had my last recorder lesson about two years before this.'

Baur's *Incontri* used chords, although in essentials not avant-garde music, relying on flutter tonguing, higher pitches and more dynamics than usual. But it had served its purpose and after hearing some of Michael Vetter's most recent technical discoveries Baur wrote *62 Mutazione*, now recorded on the *Flauto Dolce ed Acerbo* record.

The next step was meeting the Dutch composer Rob du Bois, who'd already written for Frans Brueggen. So Michael Vetter offered to give Brueggen a copy of the Baur, which was not yet published, in exchange for du Bois—which they did. He became acquainted with the contemporary Dutch school, who wrote him works. His advanced recorder method, *Il Flauto Dolce ed Acerbo*, written while still at school, and now published by Moeck, sets out his attitudes and approach in an excellent preface. It begins: 'When in the 1920s the recorder was revived, having been forgotten for about 150 years, surely none of its patrons realised that the rediscovered "historical" instrument could be useful for contemporary music, especially as they themselves were mostly not too close to the modern developments. However the flauto dolce soon gained a firm place as a favourite instrument in the youth movement and in the authentic interpretation of baroque and pre-baroque music'. Michael Vetter points out that when modern composers began writing for the instrument they unconsciously and consciously modelled their works both technically and stylistically on the baroque and he describes how this approach handicapped finding the recorder's new role. Just as the major-minor key system is only part of a larger musical world so the baroque style is only part of the recorder's range. It is admirably suited to modern music: 'Within this considerable range it has dynamic possibilities which stretch from the shrill, penetrating fortissimo to the most tender, nearly inaudible harmonics. The timbre of many notes can be considerably varied by the abundance of possible fingerings. The unusually strong sensitivity to overblowing makes it possible to produce sounds, combined from tones and overtones, in which—according to breath pressure—some notes dominate, succumb or disappear. Many of these and further possibilities are in close affinity to electronic music, especially the "underblown" harmonics, the chords and chordal combinations as well as the white noise of the closed and covered registers.'

We see now the reason for the title *Flauto Dolce ed Acerbo*—the latter giving the instrument immense possibilities for producing 'musical tensions as scarcely any other instrument can . . . ' The musical examples in the book are all from this century—the only baroque piece is quoted in a modern arrangement: 'The new material, however, once discovered, provokes experiments and critical attitudes, especially as it conforms to the musical style of our time and could be helpful in forming it.' 'I hoped to get a lot of people to play like this' he said, 'I wasn't interested in being just a recorder player, nor am I today. But I did see the possibilities that lay in the recorder. No other instrument has these and if somebody said to me I could now go back and choose any instrument I would start earlier on the voice, but otherwise I wouldn't change.'

Why such stress on the voice? 'I think one has to start with the voice and not with instruments' he replied. 'The real musician

went out with his voice, helping himself with the recorder and also with electronic equipment. This was my reality.' When rehearsals started he was forced to begin with his voice, his recorders and electronic equipment having been lost en route. 'I had to *sing*' he said, 'and I wasn't even a professional singer.' Stockhausen was convinced by his vocal version and another door had opened. Michael Vetter retained his independence—Stockhausen didn't want to turn him into a pupil. He still doesn't show him his compositions but he regards Stockhausen as his best friend amongst composers.

Some concerts took place in a grotto with natural acoustics where Michael Vetter improvised *Spiral*, organising it according to the feedback (6 seconds) of the hall. '*Spiral* has to be performed with short-wave radio as the source of elementary musical material. In this version, Stockhausen suddenly spoke words (the dedication of this music to the guests of honour), instead of the radio. Reacting on him and receiving his reactions, I felt more than ever this special friendship and possibility of trusting each other on a very musical level'. Another highlight was being able to work in Expo's specially-designed auditorium. In 1955 Stockhausen outlined a plan for a spherically-shaped room provided with loudspeakers, with a transparent sound-permeable platform for listeners hanging in the middle—a vision of the ideal auditorium for electronic music. 'Financial difficulties prevented this from being completely realised,' he said. 'There had to be many compromises but it turned out to be really remarkable as it was. For the first time we could move in seven channels through the auditorium over 300 loudspeakers.'

Michael Vetter lived in Kyoto and as he had no electronic equipment with him he would practise with recorder only, going each day to a cemetery on a hillside near a pagoda, that looked towards Kyoto. 'The first time I started making music I heard so many sounds, including animals and those of the modern city that I thought I must try to integrate myself into these acoustic movements. I was really forced. It wasn't that I thought "now I will start playing with mother nature". I started to play my own music as part of this context. I began with a new method of learning my instrument. I was sitting down and busy with the technical and compositional problems, but finally just playing as if for listeners so that my practice was already a piece. I gave it the title of *Aulodien* for voice and instrument, the music being bounded by the player's personality. I discovered how to use all the fingerings I'd outlined in my method. This developed in an incredible way in Japan into a real creative process. I've now dedicated *Aulodien* to Frans Brueggen. I had to give him something important as for him I'm the most irritating person in the world on the recorder. He once called me a dilettante for baroque music though he doesn't mind me for modern.'

Japan affected him deeply—*Aulodien* had above all the incantatory quality of traditional Japanese music. He was attracted to one of their instruments, the shakuhachi, a thick bamboo pipe. 'Its music has a lot of glissando, sensible articulation and expressive sound colours' he said. 'It has much *affekt* (in the sense C. P. E. Bach used the word). The shakuhachi player is really a player, he normally doesn't sit but he moves like an actor. I saw also a very important connection with the sho-chtidici, an instrument rather like a harmonica or mouth organ which moves in chords very slowly and is able to modulate in a special Japanese way from one to the other. I was able to compare my own spontaneous invention with the history of performance in that style.'

At present Michael Vetter is writing a piece for Roy Hart called *Stimmbrüche* which depicts through the voice, especially the voice-break, the challenges and changes the human personality undergoes throughout its life.

He believes children must have the opportunity to make music first then learn about it. And he believes the recorder has already so many possibilities it is not necessary to change things: 'almost the only thing I did was to electrify the recorder—the second volume

of the Moeck tutor will demonstrate this.' He uses Moeck recorders
—'perhaps they are especially useful for new music, but I saw
good instruments from very different makers. For instance I
possess a very interesting metal recorder on which everything is
movable—it has a very big cylinder. It also gives me the chance
to move the block, which gives a lot of colour-registers.'

His attitude to the baroque is unequivocal. 'Sometimes I play
baroque music with interest, but I must confess I don't like
baroque recorder music even from my best friend Frans Brueggen.
If a violinist was on such a low technical level as most baroque
music players he wouldn't get the smallest prize. The recorder
is not intrinsically easier than the piano but the recorder player
seldom practises more than two hours a day while the pianist
spends eight. The violinist has to play Brahms, Tchaikovsky and
so on: his baroque is inspired by three centuries of music, his
sound cannot go backwards. The pity of the baroque players is that
they are without the romantic composers. They can't practise
Brahms or Schoenberg so they don't achieve a comparable kind of
sound to the violinist.'

Most twentieth-century recorder music seems old hat to him
—second hand and second-rate. He spends 20% of his time on
historical music and 80% on contemporary. Only the avant-
garde have put life into this century's recorder music. 'I have
learned to understand what is music from the nature of sounds,
from the history and topography of "art" and "folk" music, but
also from working with personalities like Stockhausen, and re-
laxing with as high-class pop-music as that from the Beatles, for
example.' 'I only play baroque when or if I can see it can express
what I want to say exactly. I must be urged to say something
which this music can say. Only if there's a really important
reason do I play an old piece. Really the only music I want to
play today is by Stockhausen and myself.'

Michael Vetter now lives in Münster with his wife, a student
of theology and pedagogy who works with children in both fields.

'My neighbours look at me as if I'm a strange animal, but I've never had any trouble even when I practise with my amplifiers at night. In Bonn I'm starting this year a teaching institute for experimental music. At first I'll have to do it alone, later with assistants, Karlheinz Böttner, my guitar player and Roy Hart. This will be linked with my work for Klett, the educational publishers, for whom I'm writing a comprehensive new method covering music from the earliest stages. It'll be the first institute of its kind anywhere. There'll be no historical subjects, just painting, photography and poetry and a lot of different improvisation-classes. There won't be many lecturers and everyone must be an excellent artist.'

Michael Vetter is an intensely dedicated personality, a primal force in the recorder world and in avant-garde music, detonating accepted assumptions and stimulating a new approach. He does not stand still for his music-making proceeds further towards answering those philosophical questions that lie behind his uncompleted thesis. Why do human beings need a theology—what is music?

Cage, John, 28
Cappella Coloniensis, 46
Cavalli, Francesco, 21
Chambers, H. A., 37
Champion, Max and Stephanie, 37
Chickering, 30
Chopin, Frédéric, 49
Clarke, Jeremiah, 14
Clemencic, René, 20ff
Clemencic Consort, 22
Collette, Joannes, 16, 17, 21, 53
Conant, Robert, 40
Conrad, Ferdinand, 24ff, 43, 46, 55, 57
Cooke, Arnold, 64
Coolsma, Hans, 18, 45
Couperin, François, 22
Cudworth, Charles, 50

Dart, Thurston, 50
Davenport, LaNoue, 27ff
Deller, Alfred, 49
Dolmetsch, Arnold, 30ff
Dolmetsch, Carl, 30ff, 37, 52
Dolmetsch, Rudolph, 31
Dorati, Antal, 42
Dowland, John, 38
Draghi, Antonio, 21
Dufay, Guillaume, 53
Dynamite, Kid, 52

Elgar, Edward, 51
Evans-Pritchard, E., 47
Eyck, Jacob van, 44

Fehr, Hans-Conrad, 45, 58
Fesch, Willem de, 18
Flesch, Carl, 31
Fortner, Wolfgang, 24
Fürtwängler, Wilhelm, 13
Fux, J. J., 23

Purcell, Henry, 13, 26, 27, 39, 51

Veracini, Francesco, 18, 26
Vetter, Michael, 63ff
Vinci, Leonardo, 57
Vivaldi, Antonio, 42, 54, 61
Voss, Elizabeth (*m.* Edgar Hunt), 37

Walter, Ronald, 60
Warmalo, Willem van, 52
Waters, Stephen, 60
Webern, Anton, 28
Wenzinger, August, 24, 43, 56